THINKING CRITICALLY
TO DEVELOP A PHILOSOPHY OF LIFE

THE GADFLY EXERCISES
from the writings of

Jerome

STANSBURY
PUBLISHING
Chico, Ca.

Thinking Critically to Develop a Philosophy of Life: The Gadfly Exercises
Copyright © 2018, 2020 by Jerome A. Dirnberger
First edition 2018. Second edition 2020

ISBN 978-1-935807-50-6 2nd ed. pbk.
ISBN 978-1-935807-37-7 1st ed. pbk
ISBN 978-1-935807-38-4 ePub
ISBN 978-1-935807-40-7 Kindle

Library of Congress Control Number: 2018932351
Second Edition

Stansbury Publishing is an imprint of
Heidelberg Graphics

All rights reserved. No part of this book may be be reproduced or transmitted in any form or by any means, electronic or mechanical, including photocopying, recording, or by any information storage and retrieval system, without permission in writing from the copyright holder or publisher, except for reviews.

THIS BOOK IS DEDICATED TO MY WIFE
ANGELA MARIA ROZO
(1958-2009)
WHO ENCOURAGED ME TO WRITE
AND ENJOYED MY WRITINGS

A gadfly is a horsefly in English terminology. Socrates is thought to have considered himself a "gadfly on the butt of society." He is known for questioning the establishment, being ironic, asking questions and emphasizing a moral code.

A PHILOSOPHY OF LIFE

WHAT IS IT?

No matter your religious beliefs, you have your own unique philosophy of life. It has three aspects: your understanding of the cosmos (the orderly universe); how to live in a community (morality, ethics); and cognizance of yourself (knowledge, awareness).

Why would you want to describe your philosophy of life? Because by setting down your priorities, it will be easier for you to make some of life's more difficult decisions especially when you compare their relative impact and importance.

In order to have a more peaceful life, you need to be aware of yourself in your surroundings, thus you will also reduce your stress and avoid getting angry. Anger is a symptom that you lack control of a situation which could have been solved by preparing yourself ahead of time for various eventualities. Being prepared, you will realize that if you are angry at someone it is only yourself, not him or her, you should control.

Later we will look at two historical persons' philosophies of life: one is Chinese philosopher Lao Tzu, who wrote the *Tao Te Ching* twenty-five hundred years ago, and the other is reformist Jewish rabbi Jesus of Nazareth, whose brother wrote down his sayings in *The Gospel of Thomas*. Both of these books are interpreted by this author into modern English and available through Amazon or *www.writingsofjerome.com*

THE COSMOS

Imagine *before* the Big Bang (or God's Creation). Pretty difficult, eh? But you probably have your own idea(s).

When we look out at night, we see gigantic space filled with billions of planets and stars. When we study the sky carefully it becomes apparent there is some sort of order. Planets are revolving around stars and stars are being born or dying. Obviously there has to be an intelligence behind it all. Stephen Hawking's theory of everything states: the universe evolves according to well-defined laws.

When we study our own planet, we realize, besides gravity, there is a cyclical order to every living thing. Each is born, grows, declines, and dies. This process is in reality a journey. While we see that some plants and animals are plentiful in one area and not in another, we don't always know the reason. But all life wants to succeed, meaning it has to be plentiful and productive.

COMMUNITY

Since we are social animals we need to live in community to survive. Even hermits need someone to take care of them for a time after they are born. For our community to thrive, its residents have to establish some sort of rules to succeed. Following all the rules to the letter would be an ideal, however we know people don't comply all the time.

The ideal community is where: everyone lives in peace and harmony; everyone respects each other;

people are generous and giving; the disadvantaged are helped; leaders are humble, listen to the people, and act selflessly; there are no wars, nor murders, nor thefts. Each person has to do his or her part to make the community succeed.

YOUR COGNIZANCE

Do you know your strengths? Your weaknesses? Your talents? Your best abilities? Why you get sad? What are your goals? How can you accomplish them? What is legacy? How do you want to be remembered? These are just some of the questions you ask yourself in order to determine the depth of your self-knowledge.

Besides being common sensical, there are many studies showing that the more self-knowledge you have, the more you can cope with life's events and the happier you become. In general, you accept your limitations, follow your passion in doing what you enjoy, and thus exceed in doing so.

JESUS OF NAZARETH'S PHILOSOPHY OF LIFE (from *The Gospel of Thomas*)

In 1945 near the Egyptian town of Nag Hammadi, two farmers found an earthen jar while digging for fertilizer. They broke open the jar and discovered thirteen manuscripts written in ancient Coptic. Included in this library, was a gospel written by Thomas who was an apostle of the Jewish rabbi, Yesu (Jesus) of Nazareth. Thomas is not a person's name but is a nickname for twin. Generally he is accepted by scholars to be the twin of Jesus.

In this Gospel, Jesus said that when you understand the cosmos better, you will realize it is also inside of yourself (5)*. And you are a part of every living thing in this the Father's Kingdom (3). In fact, even the non-living stones will show the Father's image (19). This image includes being a light which can be described as a divine connection with the cosmos (24). Jesus continued saying that he is the light of creation. A part of him exists in everything. Split a piece of wood, he is there, lift a stone, you will find him. If you truly understand this then you too can acquire the light (77). And your light will never die (85).

Jesus' view of how one should live in community is simple and straight forward. He said you should not lie or hate. Because being dishonest will eventually become obvious. Treat people how you want to be treated is always the best way to live (6). It is best that you respect other people and their culture (14). When people who disagree come together to solve problems, they will live in harmony (106). And above all, whoever possess love, will be given more. But whoever does not possess love, will be deprived of what little they even have (41).

Jesus thinks understanding his message is difficult as only one in a thousand will (23). So how much of yourself do you really know? Jesus said you are on a journey of life and understanding (42). As you grow you must continue to gain self-knowledge of being in harmony with the natural world—because when you make your eyes, hands, and feet into ones that are at one with the cosmos, you can enter into the Kingdom of the Father (22). You have become children of the light who realize the Kingdom of the Father is inside yourself; thus being able to live in peace (59).

LAO TZU' PHILOSOPHY OF LIFE (from *The Tao Te Ching*)

This book was written over twenty-five hundred years ago by the Chinese philosopher Lao Tzu who was known to be an archivist for a Chinese kingdom and then went off to live in a small village. Lao Tzu is translated to mean "Old Master" and is not a proper name.

Lao's view of the cosmos is: Before the universe was born there was something ... infinite, vast, eternal. (25) It was before time and space and before matter and energy. (21) It was the thought before creation (4) and beyond comprehension. (14) For the lack of a better word, I call it *TAO*. (25) How do I know this truth because the *Tao* is in me. (21) The *Tao* not only gives birth to all things but also nourishes, cultivates, cares for, comforts, and protects. (51)

With regard to living in community a person should strive to do good, be generous, compassionate, sincere, and give of yourself. (8) To follow the Tao, you have to perceive integrity, embrace simplicity, reduce egoism, and limit your desires. (19) Thus, a Taoist people can live in peace and greater harmony. (3)

Do the following questions make you more cognizant of yourself? In understanding your personal *yin* and *yang* can you balance them? In focusing your *ch'i* can it be as plaint as a newborn's? In clearing your mind can it be free of distractions? Can you be patient? Can you be objective? (10)

To gain more self-awareness, you must understand male attributes but emphasize the female ones. Be open to the world and aware of various cultures so that you act with humility and simplicity. (38) Thus you will become one with the ever-evolving universe. (56)

THE NEXT STEPS

Since your life is a journey, your philosophy will evolve. I suggest you write down your thoughts, comments, ideas, goals, critiques, etc. So that you can refer to them periodically when you meditate or contemplate. Use the exercises in this book to help you create your own Philosophy of Life.

*Note: Sayings of Jesus come from *The Gospel of Thomas: The Original Sayings of Jesus* from the writings of Jerome with the numbers referring to that individual saying. The quotes from the *Tao Te Ching by Lao Tzu: A twenty-first century English interpretation* by Jerome are from the book of the same name with the numbers referring to the chapter. Both books are by this author.

INTRODUCTION

The Constitution of the United States seems to be well written and easily understood. There are nine Supreme Court justices, some of the brightest people in the country, trying to interpret it. Sometimes they cannot agree on what it says. Do they think ... critically?

Over the years, I have developed scenarios, ponderings, and writings trying to help me think more critically. I pass some of these along to you in this book, not to have you agree or disagree with me, but to encourage you to develop your own reasons to some of life's most challenging questions.

Don't believe everything you hear or read at first glance. Think for yourself. You are going to need to spend time with yourself. Maybe turn off the electronics and take a quiet walk. Ask yourself a question and then answer it. It is as simple as that. Oh, sorry, I forgot, you might have to do some research by checking with the experts and other knowledgeable people in the field.

It would help for you to write down your own thoughts so you can review them over your lifetime. They will probably change, or they should change, as you gain more experience, knowledge, and wisdom.

—Jerome Dirnberger

ON BEING A (BETTER) CRITICAL THINKER

Do not try to control anyone except yourself
If you give up dominating others
You learn to respect each person

When you manage yourself
Your desires will be more moderate
And you will learn humility

Learn to identify options for solving problems
What info do I need? Which is best? And why?
Remember worry is negative while action is positive

Learn to be a citizen of the world
Study problems and solutions
From other cultures' perspectives

Study what is *news* and *entertainment*
News is history and economics
While *entertainment* is sex and violence

Understand the difference between *sex* and *love*
Between *freedom fighters* and *terrorists*
Between *collateral damage* and the *killing of innocents*

Know the difference between *faith* and *facts*
And between *believe* and *can*
Know the five most important goals of your friend

Who do you blame for the failures in your life?
Ex-spouse, lover, parents, siblings?
Ex-bosses, co-workers? friends? Or yourself?

Do not be ethnocentric, intolerant, arrogant, biased
Do read, listen, help others, reflect, evolve

CONTENTS

A Philosophy of Life 5
Introduction 11
On Being a (Better) Critical Thinker 12
The Apprentice 15
A Wise Man 16
Life's Lessons 17
Life Is Unfair 18
Improve Your Life 19
Sex, Lust, and Love 20
An Irish Tradition 21
When I Say *I Love, I* 23
The Conversation 24
Want to be Smarter? 26
When Looking in a Mirror 27
Problem or Solution? 28
On Gossip 29
What I've Learned 31
Answers to My Questions 32
Comparative Philosophy 33
How Is Man Different from Other Animals? 35
Together 36
Heroes 37
Freedom 38
Suffering 39
Is God Evil? 41
When Does Life Begin? 42
Is There Life After Death? 43
$E=Mc^2$ 45
The Soul Is to the Mind 47
Serenity 49
Santa Claus Is Coming 50
Finding Your Spirit 51
Religion Is 52

My God 53
My Ten Commandments 54
Abraham's Covenant with God 55
Which God Do You Believe In? 56
Poor Job 57
The First Holocaust 58
Who Was Jesus of Nazareth? 60
What Happened to Mary(S)? 62
The Gospel of Thomas 63
The Gospel of Mary of Magdala 66
What If? 68
The Pieta 70
The Greatest Salesman 72
The Great Conspiracy 75
The Good Ol' Boys 77
The Bar Is Too High 79
Rereading the Bible 80
Want To Be a Great Leader? 81
A Successful Army (Or Football Team) 82
Are We So Arrogant? 83
Negotiation 84
The Ten Fundamental Rights of the
   Human Condition 86
West and East 87
The People 88
All Men Are Created Equal 90
Top Secret Report 91
In the Future 92
I Heard About This Man 94
My Uncle Bill 95
My Uncle Tim 97
End of a Bureaucracy 99
Acknowledgments 101

THE APPRENTICE

A very gifted young artist works
Under a Master who realizes her talent
And starts to teach her all he knows
As he believes she will surpass him

In her spare time the apprentice
Works on her own piece doing
What she believes will be
Her masterpiece

The Master watches for many months
The progress and marvels to himself
Of the beauty and perfection of it
Which is better than he could do

The apprentice is almost finished
In a moment of lost concentration
She makes a very minor mistake
Almost invisible to the untrained eye

She puts it aside for many days
Thinking of what can she do
Finally she decides it cannot be fixed
And throws it away

The Master finds it and marvels
Then notices the imperfection and
Begins weeping over human frailty
Because it makes her Masterpiece *perfect*

A WISE MAN ...

Has a positive attitude
Has a mind that is open
Can give away possessions
Embraces silence
Is spiritual
Can envision success
Follows his passion
Realizes life is not fair
Accepts his limitations
Gives of himself

PS. Most women do not need this advice because they are already wise!

LIFE'S LESSONS

Tell your hopes to the banker, fears to your attorney
Do not talk to the police, unless you call them
You can divorce your spouse, but not your children
During times of a loss of a love, hug your children
Sometimes plan A does not work out: have a plan B
A true friend tells you what is best for you
You learn by making mistakes and accepting them
You will learn more about someone by listening
Right is tight, left is loose
Measure twice, cut once
Do not completely trust your doctor: do research
When driving a car, look a hundred yards down the road
With every paycheck, put some into savings
When trying to sell, listen to the customer's needs
Ask questions. ... who, what, where, when, why
Feeling depressed? go help someone in need
Be generous: you will be paid back with more
Spend some time alone to meditate or contemplate
Excel at something for which you have a passion

LIFE IS UNFAIR

You will be disappointed, even despair
You will be treated unfairly and unjustly
You will be betrayed and ridiculed

If you have money, people will try to steal it
If you are popular, people will tell lies about you
If you love, your lover will reject you

Be careful of the "holier than thou" people
Watch out for the "if it's too good to be true"
Stand firm against the "if you love me …"

So now there are no surprises
Accept it, move on
Be loyal to your family

Be true to your friends
The ones who do what is best for you and
Work to improve the lives of the disadvantaged

IMPROVE YOUR LIFE

OK, do you want to improve your life?
Pick any five of the following
But only one to do each year

Live where you like
Work only if it is fun
Work really hard in your twenties
Live under your means
Teach your child to laugh
Volunteer to help others
Be physically active
Spend time meditating
Be a true friend
Be inquisitive
Read to be a critical thinker
Marry the love of your life
Respect other's views

SEX, LUST, AND LOVE

Ok, so now you are a teenager
Welcome to the real world
Of becoming an adult
    Your body is changing
    And your hormones are raging
    So you want to know about *sex*
This is the physical part
Of reproduction of our species
Where man and woman join together
    The process is called intercourse
    As the man's penis enters
    The woman's vagina
Your first exploratory actions
Of learning your own body
Are normal, and this is sex
    Sexual activity with another person
    In your teenage years
    Is *lust*
When another person pressures you
To have sexual activity
To satisfy their own desires
    What you really should
    Aim for is *love*
    Which requires another kind of intercourse
Namely, the communication between
Two persons to get to know each other
Before making love
    Both kinds of intercourse
    Require sharing and caring
    It is rewarding and can last a lifetime

AN IRISH TRADITION

There is an Irish tradition which states
On the feast of Imbolc you can divorce your spouse
Just by saying the "contract is broken"

However this annual event could be
A good catalyst for self-analysis and
Making the necessary improvements

Have you grown closer or further apart?
Do you complain about your spouse to others?
Do you get angry because you are not in control?

Remember when passion was the first stage
And how important it was to revel in the chemistry
Of physical attraction and to simply enjoy life

Then came love, which is the bond
Between individuals that signifies
They care for each other and the union itself

Finally came commitment, being the most difficult stage
As you have to continually compromise
And learn the important priorities of the union

While no union is perfect
It does take selflessness to make it better
But the benefits are worth it

There is a time to be cared for, and a time to be caring
There is a time to be caressed, and a time to caress
There is a time to speak, and a time to be silent
There is a time to cry, and a time to be comforted
There is a time to work, and a time to play

There is a time to spend, and a time to save
There is a time to be together, and a time for being alone
There is a time to give, and a time to take
There is a time of joy, and a time of sorrow
There is a time to be angry, and a time to laugh
There is always time to hold hands
There is always time to communicate honestly
There is always time to be respectful

WHEN I SAY *I LOVE*, I ...

enjoy sex,
commit to my work,
have concern for my friends,
respect my parents,
care for my children,
compromise in my marriage,
am passionate to my true self,
show compassion to my enemies,
am at one with the godhead.

THE CONVERSATION

Have you had "the conversation" with your children?
You know, the one about "sex"
Or perhaps the one about "death"

Maybe it is easier and more important to discuss
"love" and "friendship" rather than "sex"
And "quality of life" rather than "death"

Sex and death are merely physical activities
While love, friendship, and quality of life
Are human, even spiritual elements

Your children need a foundation on which
To build their values and mores
And make their own decisions

Your children need to know about
Your experiences, your successes, your mistakes
So tell them your stories

Who are your friends ... and why?
Was your first love your friend ... and still now?
Why do people fall out of love?

How important is communication?
How do you gain a person's trust and loyalty?
Should you be open about your feelings?

Did anyone break your heart?
How did you handle the pain?
Is family more important than friends?

What is it like to have a loved-one pass on?
Where does a person go after he or she dies?
Why does the loss feel so bad?

Can a person live too long?
If a person wants to die, can you help him or her?
Am I responsible for caring for my parents?

Obviously, this is a continuing conversation

WANT TO BE SMARTER?

While conversing, look people in the eye
When reading, look up unknown words
While hiking, identify bird songs
When running, relax
While driving, observe the road a quarter mile ahead
Take a photo, sing a song, or paint a picture.

WHEN LOOKING IN A MIRROR

If you are short
   Do you see yourself as taller?

If you are fat
   Do you see yourself as thinner?

If you are not good looking
   Do you see yourself as handsome?

Or how about ...

Do you think yourself to be generous?
Do you think yourself to be honest?
Do you think yourself to be religious?
Do you think yourself to be compassionate?

    Maybe not

PROBLEM OR SOLUTION?

In times of crisis
In times of stress
In times of tragedy

   When families grieve
   When friends are concerned
   When loved ones are affected

      You can become withdrawn
      You can accuse others
      You can think only of your own needs

      OR

      You can come together
      You can empathize
      You can be selfless

ON GOSSIP

The priest decided to preach on Sunday
About the commandment. ... Not to bear false witness
Against your neighbor ... so don't lie or gossip

He said that since Jesus loves EVERY ONE
When you tell something mean about another
You are also hurting Jesus' feelings

This resonated with one of the older women
Who, in fact, was the town's gossip
Although she believed herself to be saintly

The next week, she decided to confess
To the priest about her small transgressions
Of speaking badly about her son-in-law

The priest knew who was admitting her sins and
For her penance, she could speak only good things
Plus say five 'Hail Marys'

The old woman could not stop her gossiping
So she confessed her sins again the next week
And this made her feel better, but she did not stop

After a few more times, the priest decided on a new
    penance
Which was for her to take an old pillow to her roof
Cut a hole in it and send the feathers to the wind

When she returned the following week
After confessing her gossips, the priest told her
Go throughout the town and pick up all the feathers

Then each day for the rest of her life
She could be seen walking around town
picking up feathers off the ground ... quietly

WHAT I'VE LEARNED ...

to read from school,
to think from reading,
to meditate from thinking,
to know myself from meditating,
to understand my part in the universe
    from knowing myself,
to laugh at myself from understanding my
    part in the universe.

ANSWERS TO MY QUESTIONS

FINALLY, I am dead ...
For most of my life I have had questions
But I could not find the answers

NOW ... I seek the answers to my top ten questions ...

Am I conscious?

What form is my existence?

Since I do not have senses, how do I learn?

Can I communicate with the Supreme Intelligence?

Can I communicate with my twin brother?

The rest of my family too? Angela?

Am I able to envision the past and/or the future?

Who and where is Jesus of Nazareth?

Where are Hitler and Stalin?

To what extent did my good deeds correspond to my current situation?

COMPARATIVE PHILOSOPHY

In the Bhagavad-Gita freedom comes from being
 disciplined
And being detached from material things.
Understanding the world and your place in it
Leads to acting wisely.
But the fatal flaw of the Hindu philosophy is
The idea of caste and duty.

Aristotle believed that living well
Should be the goal of everyone's life.
And to do this one needs to be virtuous,
Have practical wisdom, and be moral.
Happiness would be your reward
Only if you share it with others.

From Job, we learn bad things happen
To innocent people who are not harming others
Job believes this is God's will and
We should not question Him

A Stoic wants to control his/her anger
Because it is a symptom of lacking control
Through rational thinking you can understand the
 world,
It's cycle of birth to death, so don't be fearful.

The Buddha awakens to find life is all about suffering
While you are but a small part of the ever-changing
 universe,
And a Taoist sees the universe as an evolving cycle
To greater harmony if we respect everyone and
 everything.

So no matter what you believe
May you "live long and prosper"
And "may the Force be with you"

HOW IS MAN DIFFERENT FROM OTHER ANIMALS?

Requires longer nurturing time
Can use complex language
Is aware of own consciousness
Possesses freedom (free will) to choose
Has knowledge of life's cycles
Believes in a God/Creator/Force
Is cognizant that evil is bad

TOGETHER

Whether it is the Native Americans in the 17th century
Or the Bavarians in the 18th century
Or the Montanans in the 19th century
The rural life is one of commitment and dedication

To the land and animals for sustenance
To the family for support
To the Creator for blessings

The land is not seen as needing ownership
But rather as a legacy to pass on to future generations
So it must be left in better shape than it was found

The family is the most important element in the equation
For without the hard work and productivity of each member
It is the only way to survive both the joys and sorrows of life

The Creator provides the opportunities and blessings
For the family and the land to live in harmony
Together

HEROES

Do you want to understand a person or a people?
Then ask them to describe their heroes
And why they admire their hero

The culture of a tribe or group or society
Can be changed by providing the children
With new legends, stories, or myths

For me, the Lone Ranger rode around the lawless West
With his faithful Indian companion, Tonto
And brought the bad guys to justice without killing them

For my children, Luke Skywalker was able to find within himself
The Force which is the connection of all peaceful people
And used it to combat the evil forces in the universe

A hero should be a model for humility, compassion,
Action against bias, prejudice, materialism, and corruption
And should possess a willingness to die for his or her beliefs

Some heroes become religious idols, like Jesus and Mohammed
Whose message gets corrupted by pseudo-heroes
So beware of those who preach death and violence to non-believers

FREEDOM

Freedom is all about choices

The awareness to understand their ramifications
The strength to act on the ones you choose
The discipline to carry them out

Freedom requires making the best choices

The best choices for you are ones
That will assist you to evolve to a greater awareness
Of what is also best for our species and our planet

Most other species inherently adapt to change
As their motivation is food, security, and reproduction
Because of our intelligence we have a duty to help

Only when there is a great natural disaster
Or when we humans act in self interests
Do intelligence and freedom regress

SUFFERING

Each person is able to suffer to the depths of their soul
With each soul having a different degree of maturity
Depending upon the amount of suffering it endures

No soul reaches full maturity
As that entails all the knowledge
Of the universe, which is God or the Tao

We suffer because we have loved
For when we lose a person we love
We suffer depending on the depth of that love

Take for example, Jesus of Nazareth
Who loved his mother, father, family, friends,
Disciples, Mary of Magdala, and children

Before he started his ministry
He spent a month in the desert
Mediating on his life and what to do

I think it was because he suffered a recent loss
Maybe his father passed after a long illness
He had to have been very close to him

He was the eldest son
Following in the same trade as
They worked shoulder to shoulder every day

Or maybe earlier, he lost his wife and a child
As it was the Jewish custom for men to marry
He would have been looked upon as strange if he did not

Jesus is said to have loved little children and
Their parents would not have let them go
To a strange man

Remember what Khalil Gibran wrote long ago that
The deeper that sorrow carves into your being
The more joy you can contain

IS GOD EVIL?

What we see, feel, hear, smell, and breathe plus
What we cannot see, feel, hear, smell, and breathe
Is ALL a part of the Creator

The Creator is known by His/Her Creation
So everything that IS, is a part of the Creator
Then since evil exists, Is not God evil?

But, I believe, evil is an invention of man
Evil is not normal unintended injury, pain, death
These are all a part of living

Evil is action against the innocent and defenseless
Whether it be physical, emotional, or mental
That causes undeserved suffering

Evil is done by persons
Who choose to control or dominate others
And do so because they are selfish

Since the Creator rewards right order
Men and societies that live morally
In the end survive and grow

But since evil is an invention of man
Man has the power to eliminate evil
But only when each person does

WHEN DOES LIFE BEGIN?

When does life begin?
Of course, at fertilization
When the sperm hits the egg

But for human beings?
Life begins at first breath
Because we cannot live without oxygen

As Genesis says, the Lord God
Breathed into his nostrils the breath of life
And man became a living human being

Do we celebrate the anniversary
Of conception or birth?

Do we name the baby
At conception or birth?

Do we bury the miscarried fetus
Or the stillborn
Or the infant once he or she has breathed?

When is it that we die
At decomposition
Or at our last breath?

IS THERE LIFE AFTER DEATH?

Is there life after death?
Most people believe so,
But does it really matter?

The greater question is, why does our human species deserve it?
To be equal with the Creator by existing for all eternity?
Do intelligent species on other planets have the same benefit?

We have not kept our commitments to respect God and his creation
And we have murdered millions of our species in God's name
Why would God reward us with everlasting life?

    Missionaries have used the idea of *heaven*
    As an enticement for the poor and lower classes
    To survive their difficult and hard lives

Some extremists have used *paradise*
    To give the naively hopeless some hope
    If they commit martyrdom by doing their will

    Other leaders have used the fear of *hell*
    To control the behavior of their followers
    To act and believe according to their wishes

    If people need a second, third, or fourth chance
    In order to learn how to lead a virtuous life
    Then *reincarnation* is their answer

Yet the message of *authentic* spiritual leaders
Is for all people to do good and avoid evil
By respecting and helping others

Thus immortality for each person
Is the sum of his or her good and bad deeds
That continue to have effects beyond their life

$E=mc^2$

What we know is called *facts*
What we don't know is called *fiction*
What we think we know is called *beliefs*

We know there is a relationship, $E=mc^2$
Between energy and mass (e.g. our bodies)
But we don't know ALL the facts about this formula

We know that mass (m) has three dimensions
Of height, width, and depth
While speed of light (c) has one of time

But does energy (E) have a dimension?
Since "m" can be converted to "E"
After death, do our bodies convert to "E"?

What of our minds?
Or better, of our souls or spirits?
Have they always been Energy?

I have a belief
My God is the Creator
The Creator is Energy

I have a belief
I exist after death
As "E", some part of God

I have a belief
I will not have an eternal existence
Rather one for a given period of time

I will be immortal by memories of others
And the results of my words, works, and deeds
Plus by my and my ancestors' DNA

THE SOUL IS TO THE MIND

The soul is to the mind
As the heart is to the body
Bio-chemical cells provide one's personality

The soul's organs include
Reason, free will, conscious, intuition,
Happiness, goodness, justice, conscience

In animals, instincts dominate their behavior
In humans, it is the soul that rules
And it is always evolving

As the body desires a long, healthy life
The soul seeks wisdom as its goal
With wisdom being the right order of the universe

While the soul is imbued
With knowledge of this harmony
It needs greater self-awareness to mature

Jesus thought there are
Spiritual resources within every one
Because persons are made in God's image

So everyone should strive to know oneself
Thus becoming more aware
Of God's presence in His Kingdom on earth

Greater self-awareness not only comes
Through the senses, thoughts, and communication
But mainly through reflection and meditation

Gilgamesh realized he was
Not only a mortal individual
But also a part of society

So as John Donne says
No man is an island,
He is a piece of the continent

Society wants to operate in harmony
Plus man has to behave morally
Both are evolving to greater wisdom

SERENITY

Serenity can only be achieved
After loving someone very deeply
And then losing that person

Serenity can only be achieved
By journeying to the depths of depression and then
Being aware that your capacity to love is greater

Serenity can only be achieved
By feeling you are alone and sorry for yourself
And then accepting the loss

Serenity can only be achieved
By realizing it is ok to feel sadness
But knowing you are really not alone

Serenity can only be achieved
By being in harmony with life
And understanding the promise of the future

Serenity can only be achieved
By knowing there will be new experiences
With a chance to share a new love

SANTA CLAUS IS COMING

According to the old Christmas carol
"He knows if you've been bad or good
So be good for goodness sake!"

Goodness should be the goal of society
Man being a social animal
Cannot be good just by himself

Each individual has to strive
To exhibit correct moral behavior
In order to achieve a healthy society

Each individual's motivation
Has to be one of selflessness or
Caring about the other

The reward is not eternal life
But rather a well-ordered society
And happiness for the individual

Respect is the measure
Of this selflessness
Which shows a wise and healthy person

Plato believed that
God is Good and
Goodness is infinite

On the other hand being selfish
Shows a person to be unhealthy
So be good for GOoDness sake!

FINDING YOUR SPIRIT

Do you know your *spirit*?
Well, it is not your *personality*
That is how you act to others

It's not whether you are an introvert or an extrovert
Nor whether you are passive or dominant
Nor whether you are disorganized or detail-minded

No, it is not your *soul* either
The soul is the compass between right and wrong
Its depth grows with increased self-awareness

If you don't know your spirit
Be like the natives, do a vision-quest
Or like the aborigines, do a walkabout

Your spirit is the uniqueness that is YOU
It is the passion of what you wish to do or say
In connection with other humans

It will evolve because of your experiences
It will mature with your self-knowledge
It will deepen as your love does

You can see it in someone's eyes, a light
You can hear it in someone's voice, an excitement
You can feel it in someone's touch, a warm strength

RELIGION IS ...

a human invention
to answer the unanswerable
    and explain the unexplainable

a sacred place for believers
   to hear myths of their superhuman heroes
and communicate with them

a system for believers
   to know what to think
     and to guide how they act

MY GOD

My God does not have a gender
   but if IT did
      it would be both male and female.

My God does not have feelings
   but if IT did
      it would both love and hate.

My God does not interfere
   because if IT did
      there would only be good not evil.

My God is lawful
   because if IT were not
      societies would not exist.

My God is intelligent
   because if IT were not
      the universe would not be organized.

My God exists as Energy (E)
   because nothing dies
      everything just changes form ($E=mc^2$).

MY TEN COMMANDMENTS

Learn by reading, listening, and meditating

Embrace good and detest evil

Act and think positively

Take responsibility for your actions

Always do your best and give more than expected

Respect all living things

Risk loving to the depth of your soul

Treat other human beings as you wish to be treated

Share yourself, knowledge, wealth, and experiences

Honor God Whoever It is

ABRAHAM'S COVENANT WITH GOD

Terah, Abraham's father, was an artisan
Who, according to Jubilees, made idols
For his neighbors to worship as gods

Abraham rejected these gods for their lack of spirit
He wanted to worship the God Who created everything
And Who controls the rain, the sun, and the moon

Abraham's God is Almighty (el Shaddai) and
He is the Most High God (el Elyon) and
He is the Creator (Yahweh)

Who can control future events and
Reveals himself to Abraham.
Yahweh becomes the God of Israel

What Abraham wants most of all is
To be a father to many people
And to provide a land for his descendants

He has acquired a beautiful, loyal wife
Along with many followers and servants,
Plus he was very rich in cattle, in silver, and in gold

For all this, God the Almighty requires Abraham
To acknowledge Him and worship Him at various altars
Plus Abraham and his descendants have to obey His will

Abraham and God agreed to this covenant
And it is sealed in the blood of circumcision

So, how will Abraham's descendants know God's will?
How will they know they are communicating with the
  real God?

WHICH GOD DO YOU BELIEVE IN?

For Abraham, God was *El Shaddai*
He is the Almighty God of the High Mountain
He makes covenants
And makes Abraham the father of many nations

For Melchizedek, God was *El Elyon*
He is the Most High God
Creator of heaven and earth
And controls the world

For the Israelites, God was *Elohim*
He is the Everlasting God
Who watches over Israel
And is to be revered and worshiped

For Moses, God was Yahweh
He is the Living God, *He who is*
He is the creator and judge
Who imposes his will upon man and history

For Jesus, God was the *Father*
He lives in heaven but cares about his children
He is the model of love and perfection
Who demands that everyone live a moral life

For Paul, God was the *Lord Jesus Christ*
Because he was crucified and resurrected
For the salvation of all believers
Or face damnation for the non-believers

POOR JOB

Job has worked long and hard
He believes he is a faithful servant of God
Hhe is blessed with wealth and a large family

But is his faith in God
The basis for his good fortune?
What would happen if he lost it all?

Then one of God's emissaries destroys Job's animals
And later he kills Job's children
But Job remains loyal and faithful to God!

So the emissary decides to test Job further
He strikes Job with great physical pain
But Job remains loyal and faithful to God!

Job's friends try to comfort him
But surely Job must have done something evil
To bring about all these problems

Job declares he is not guilty of anything wrong
He is innocent, someone else is guilty
In his grief, he curses the day he was born

Finally God declares that He should not be blamed
After all ... He is above questioning and judgment
He is Creator ... His actions are unknowable to man

The Lord gives, and the Lord takes away. ...
Blessed be the name of the Lord

THE FIRST HOLOCAUST

When Moses led his people out of Egypt
Not all the local inhabitants welcomed them through
    their land
Both kings, Sihon of the Amorites and Og of Mathnin,
Tried to protect their people and their lands

However, the Israelites smote them, their sons,
And all their people, even the children
Until there was not a survivor left
Then the Israelites possessed the land

Against Midian, the Israelites slew all the males
And took all the women as captives plus their little ones
And all the cattle, their flocks, and all their wealth
The Israelites plundered and kept for themselves.

Moses questioned why they let the women and children
    live,
So the Israelites killed every male among the little ones
And killed every woman who had known man
But the rest of the females, they kept for themselves.

Finally Joshua and the Israelites crossed the Jordan River
Into the land promised by God to Abraham
Where they destroyed Jericho, including men and
    women,
Young and old, plus oxen, sheep, and asses.

Then the Israelites burned the city with fire,
And all that was therein,
Only silver and gold and vessels of brass and iron
They brought in to the treasury of the Lord's house.

When the Israelites had finished slaying all the inhabitants of Ai
In the fields and in the wilderness where they were pursued
The Israelites returned to Ai and smote it with the edge of the sword
So it was that 12,000 men and women fell that day.

Later Joshua captured Makkar
And he slew the king and all the persons in it
He left none remaining
And so with Libnah, Lachish, Gezer, Eglon, and Hebron

Joshua then returned to Debir
And captured it, its king, and all its towns
The Israelites smote them with edge of the sword
And utterly destroyed all the persons

THE ISRAELITES LEFT NONE REMAINING

WHO WAS JESUS OF NAZARETH?

Jesus was a Jew who was born and raised in a small town
Which was on a trade route in which diverse peoples passed.
Thus he became knowledgeable of other's beliefs.
As a boy he was required to study Jewish laws
And developed into a thoughtful, observant, and wise man.
In his day there were many who suffered and were very poor
Primarily as a result of the Roman rule and the wealthy (religious) class.
Having several brothers and sisters
He enjoyed children and they liked him.
As a young man he learned and worked a skilled trade.
He had a long intimate relationship with his companion, Mary of Magdala.
In later years he went on a "vision quest" in the desert
Where he decided to be a teacher (*rabbi*)
With the desire to reform Judaism.
Using a unique style of telling stories (parables)
He developed his idea of the *Kingdom of God*
Where people lived the *Sermon on the Mount.*
By emphasizing doing good works and
Avoiding the actions which degrade relationships
They would reap the rewards of a better life.
All the while Jesus lived the life he preached.
He had great charisma and the ability to heal.

While he honored and praised God (*Abba*)
His opposition of paying for Temple sacrifices
Got him killed.
Jesus did not say he was God

Nor did he intend to start a new religion.
That was left up to Paul to develop one
Who with his experiences and knowledge based on
 Greek, Roman, and Jewish philosophy and culture.

Jesus' disciples had a "'vision" of him alive
After his crucifixion and death
Thus motivating them to continue his mission.

WHAT HAPPENED TO MARY(S)?

While Jesus called his God, "Father" (*Abba*)
He respected both men and women equally
But the two Mary's were closer to him than any man.

Mary, the mother of Jesus, taught her eldest son
   compassion for all,
Encouraged his religious studies,
And experienced the ordeal of watching him die.

She was with him during his ministry to the unfortunate
She was with him in his rebellion to bring about a new
   order
She was with him in his suffering and crucifixion

She was at the first meeting of the new movement
When they elected another apostle to replace Judas
And where Simon Peter took control.

Mary of Magdala was said to be Jesus' intimate
   companion
She explained his vision of the Kingdom of God
To the disciples when they did not understand.

She was a witness to his crucifixion and death
She was a witness to his burial
She was a witness to his empty tomb and apparition

Yet, she and his mother were shut out of the movement.
   why?
Oh, how different Christianity would look today if they
   had been involved,
Maybe, more like Jesus' vision of the Kingdom of God.

THE GOSPEL OF THOMAS

Thomas (Aramaic) or *Didymus* (Greek) means *twin*
Thomas (the twin) is another Judas, a brother of Jesus
According to the Eastern Church he is Jesus' twin
 brother
Who became the Apostle to India

This gospel is one of the first writings about Jesus
And it is said to have two parts
One composed by Jesus' brother, Judas (Thomas)
And the other by another brother, James

When the disciples ask Jesus who is to be their leader
He responds to go to James the Just, this brother
But in the synoptic gospels, Peter is the leader
And in the Acts of the Apostles, it is Paul

The brothers in Thomas' gospel describe
Jesus' philosophy and message
They do not mention his miracles
Nor his passion, nor his resurrection

Some of the sayings are what parents would teach their
 children
Good persons produce and say good
Bad persons produce and say evil
From the wickedness in their hearts

Be adaptable and respectful to other people
When you go into different regions
And when people invite you in
Eat what they serve you

When you see a sliver in your friend's eye
But you don't see the one in your own
You must first take out yours
Then you will see well enough to remove your friend's

Don't worry every day from morning to evening
About what you are going to wear or eat
You are better than the lilies of the field
And they are taken care of

Give to the emperor what is his
And to God what belongs to Him
Or how about, be as sly as snakes
And as simple as doves

Love your brother like your own soul
Guard him like the pupil of your eye
Plus if a blind man leads a blind man
They will both fall into a pit

What is unique to Jesus' message in this gospel is
His view of the kingdom of God (imperial rule)
And the key to understanding this kingdom
Is recognizing your affinity with God

Jesus says of himself, I am the light before all things
I am all things; from me all things come forth
Split a piece of wood, I am there
Lift a stone, you will find me

We are all made in the image of God
Which is hidden within everyone
But if you become a child
You will know the kingdom is in you

The kingdom is inside you, and outside you
When you know yourself
You will know the depth of things
That you are a child of the living Father

The kingdom is like a mustard seed
The smallest of all seeds
When it falls on prepared soil
It grows to a large plant and shelters the birds

The Father's imperial rule is like the trader
Who had a lot of merchandise
When he found a pearl
He sold other items and bought the pearl

The Father's imperial rule is like a woman
Who took a little leaven
Mixed it with dough
And made large loaves of bread

The kingdom will not come by waiting for it
It is not a matter of saying "here it is" or "there it is"
Rather, the kingdom is spread out upon the earth
And men do not see it

THE GOSPEL OF MARY OF MAGDALA

Mary of Magdala is the Apostle to the Apostles
She is more spiritually mature than the others
And is capable of teaching them Jesus' message

In Jesus' teaching, the *Son of Man*
Or *the Child of True Humanity*
Exists within every person

Within each person there is the truth
The image of *the Kingdom of God*
Or *the Divine Realm*

You have to seek within yourself
To find the true knowledge
That overcomes worldly attachments

Sin is the passion
Of following worldly desires
And turning away from God

To attain salvation
The immortal soul has to journey through the material world
Of ignorance, arrogance, jealousy, and desire

To reach God who is Good(ness)
You have to have knowledge of the Divine Realm
Where there is light, peace, and love

After Jesus' departure, the apostles
Have not fully understood his message
And are reluctant to leave to preach the gospel

Some are still attached to earthly passions
Like Peter who remains jealous, envious, and angry
The others ask Mary to teach them

And she does

WHAT IF? ...

What if ... Josephus' description of John the Baptizer was accurate? As Josephus stated "a good man and had urged the Jews to exert themselves to virtue, both as to justice toward one another and reverence towards God, and having done so join together in washing. For immersion in water, it was clear to him, could not be used for the forgiveness of sins, but as a sanctification of the body, and only if the soul was already thoroughly purified by right actions"?

What if ... Jesus, who was known to be a follower of John's, agreed to this message and made it one of the central themes to his own?

What if ... Jesus was a "normal" man of his time and culture in that he had married, maybe had a child, worked as a successful tradesman and saved enough money to allow not only himself but his mother to join him in traveling to deliver his message?

What if ... Jesus was a man who had experienced traumatic events in his life, like the death of his father, death of his wife and stillborn child (all normal occurrences for his society) that made him a more deeply spiritual person?

What if ... Jesus being a normal man had a close relationship with Mary of Magdala?

What if ... One of Jesus' main purposes was to get his listeners to think by using parables and aphorisms rather than explicit descriptions on how to live?

What if ... Some of Jesus' followers were not smart enough to understand some of his sayings and asked someone who did, namely Mary of Magdala, to explain?

What if ... Jesus' bodily resurrection did *not* occur as we understand that concept from today's perspective?

What if ... Jesus had appeared to his mother FIRST before anyone else; I mean she bore him, she raised him, she traveled with him, she watched him suffer and die, she probably held his dead body (like Michelangelo's Pieta)?

What if ... ALL the gospels written about Jesus include BOTH facts and fiction, or better yet, agenda items?

What if ... There is no after-life, as Jesus never said there was? Nor that he was the *Son of God*?

What if ... Jesus' view of God as *Father* was different than Abraham's God?

What if ... Paul was ALL WRONG in that he developed his own theology, because he felt guilty having killed innocent people and thus hoped for forgiveness and salvation, rather than having, as he said, GOD talks to him?

Would you still follow this man, Jesus?

THE PIETA

Mary is holding her dead son, Jesus, on her lap
After the body has been taken down from the cross
In terrible pain she looks at him, why him? why me?

A mother's worst nightmare
Has to be experiencing the death of her child
But more so, if the child has suffered

Growing up I heard my mother say many times
That she wanted to be the first to pass on
As she could not imagine seeing one of her sons die

In 1967 her warrior son was wounded in Vietnam
She went to the Manila hospital to comfort him
Until he died, then she gave up her desire to live

Mary raised a caring, compassionate son
At times she was a part of the group that followed him
Watching him heal others with his words and actions

The Jewish people admired and respected him
His message kept gaining more and more followers
Mary had done a great job of raising this son

Can you imagine her shock when he was arrested?
But you cannot imagine the terrible pain of
Having to watch his torture, crucifixion, and death

Her grief had to be overwhelming
She had to be physically exhausted
And emotionally spent

So why? . . . why would Jesus
Knowing his dear mother who had suffered so much
Not comfort her first after his resurrection?

THE GREATEST SALESMAN

Every good salesman needs a lot of self-confidence
He or she has to convince people of their abilities
And has to pitch a message they truly believe in

Long ago, there lived an Israelite
From the tribe of Benjamin, a Pharisee,
As Saul of Taurus boasts of himself

He was righteous
He was blameless before the law
He surpassed his peers in knowledge

Now Saul was so adamant of his beliefs, like other Pharisees,
That he took violent offense to anyone who differed
Especially the followers of Jesus who he persecuted

He even thought all women were inferior
They should not be allowed leadership roles nor speak in public
Plus all wives should be subservient to their husbands

As you know, Jesus criticized the Pharisees
For their hypocrisy and narrow-mindedness
And definitely thought women were equal

But Jesus was a rebel
Who wanted a renewed Judaism
With justice and mercy for *all*

One day Saul decided on a new path
Because he says God personally told him to
And to change his name to Paul

While he did not know Jesus when he was alive
He says that the risen Jesus
Appeared to him not in a vision but in person

He got a lot of information in this appearance
As he headed off to Arabia for the next three years
(I guess to formulate his message)

Upon his return he preached a message
Based on sin, salvation, and forgiveness
(I guess he felt guilty about his past)

Then he went to Jerusalem for two weeks
To meet with James, who was Jesus' brother, and Peter
(I guess to learn about Jesus' message of loving and caring)

Paul then spends the rest of his life travelling
Preaching his theology and brags about enduring hardships;
Torture, ship wrecks, thirst, hunger, being naked and cold

He suffers all these physical calamities with dignity
Because, as he boasted, he had excellent physical abilities and
Superior intellectual talents

Now every good salesman has a hook
To grab the listeners so they buy your pitch
But as Paul vaunted he had two. . .

If you don't believe him, then you won't have immortal life with God
and
He was always right because his power came from God

THE GREAT CONSPIRACY

The missing body of Jesus from his tomb
After his crucifixion and death
Was a great surprise to his followers

Mary of Magdala thought someone had stolen the body
Simon saw the empty tomb and went away wondering
The disciples were fearful, mourning, and weeping

Now enter Cleopah and Kepa (I Cor 15:5)
Two hitherto unknown disciples
Who came up with "the story"

While they were walking on their way to Emmaus
And talking about all the things that had happened
A stranger came up and asked them about their discussion

The stranger, later recognized as Jesus, said to them,
Did not Christ have to suffer all this to enter his glory?
Then he interpreted all the scriptures concerning himself

Only from understanding the scriptures
That Jesus had to rise from the dead,
Did he become the Christ, the Son of God

Why did Jesus appear to these two unknown disciples?
Where there not two more important disciples
To whom he might reveal this greatest mystery of all time?

Maybe, just maybe, these two made up this story
And removed the body of Jesus from the tomb
And told Mary of Magdala that Jesus had risen

Why?
To become more accepted and more important
Among the followers
An age-old motive
And they changed history

THE GOOD OL' BOYS

Peter, Paul, and other men
Are considered the founders
And *Fathers* of the Catholic religion

Peter was jealous, arrogant, hot-tempered
And betrayed Jesus not once, but three times
And criticized Mary of Magdala for being a woman

Paul says that women should not only be submissive
But also subservient to their husbands
Because women are created for men

Andrew, Peter's brother, defends him
In attacking Mary of Magdala
For her loving and teaching relationship with Jesus

Tertullian is shocked to see women doing
Men's work of teaching, preaching, and baptizing
He calls them heretics

Bishop Irenaeus is self-righteous
He orders all books destroyed
With which he does not agree

Athanasius, Bishop of Alexander,
Agrees that all books that he says are not "divine"
Should be burned because they are heretical

Emperor Constantine orders heretics
To stop meeting and surrender their property
He burnt to death Jews as they were killers of Jesus

In summary, these men are biased against women
Arrogant in that they alone know the truth
Prejudiced against other races and religious ideas

Luckily, the man who started it all
Namely Jesus of Nazareth,
Had none of those traits

THE BAR IS TOO HIGH

When Jesus commanded everyone to
Love your neighbor as yourself
He told the story of the Good Samaritan

Of love someone who is afflicted,
No matter his or her race, creed, or color,
By liquidating your assets to help him or her

For 2000 years Christians, especially Catholics,
Have failed in this regard. Just look at their history
Of religious wars, persecutions, subjections,
And genocide

In the New World, natives were slaughtered
In Africa, natives were sold into slavery
In Latin America, oligarchies rule to this day

Jesus set the bar too high!
Let's not try to love our neighbor!
Let's just learn to respect him or her!

Let each Christian respect each and all peoples
Let there no longer be prejudice, nor bias,
Nor superiority, nor arrogance, nor abuse

Let each Christian be a Good Samaritan
Because whatever you do to the least, you do to Jesus

What if the Christians change the third world. . .

What if Christian churches built schools?
What if Christian peoples built infrastructure?
What if Christian businesses built factories?

REREADING THE BIBLE

To make the Bible relevant for the modern world
Take the synoptic gospels (Luke, Matthew, Mark)
And make the following changes in the text

Replace the word *Temple* with *Vatican*
Replace the word *Pharisees* with *Ministers*
Replace the word *Sadducees* with *Priests*

Replace the word *son of man* with *human being*
Replace the word *Samaritan* with *Palestinian*
Replace the word *messiah* with *reformer*

Replace the word *son of god* with *a religious person*
Replace the word *Sanhedrin* with *College of Cardinals*
Replace the word *High Priest* with *Pope*

Jesus of Nazareth was a simple tradesman
Who wanted to reform the corrupt Judaism
And have Jews live in a respectful society

He believed God to be like his father
And wanted everyone to care for the disadvantaged
And not be hypocritical in their religious and secular life

WANT TO BE A GREAT LEADER?

You have to have the desire to learn
Especially about history
And the lives and thoughts of great leaders

You have to be a critical thinker
Especially to listen
And to think about foreign ideas

You have to be secure in yourself
Especially to know
When others have a different agenda

You have to have emotional intelligence
Especially to handle your emotions
In very stressful situations

You have to be able to love deeply
Especially to have the compassion needed
To help the unfortunates

You have to have intolerance
Especially of prejudice and bias
As they reflect ignorance

You have to give honor
Especially to God, parents, and country
So that you walk humbly

A SUCCESSFUL ARMY (OR FOOTBALL TEAM)

Has a positive attitude and team spirit
Respects the individual warrior
Is physically in excellent shape
Is able to focus its concentration
Makes up for mistakes together
Is quick in offense and aggressive in defense
Knows its opponents' strengths and weaknesses
Goes with its own strengths against its opponents' weaknesses
Performs a surprise maneuver

ARE WE SO ARROGANT?

Looking up at the stars on a clear night
We cannot see all the trillions of other stars
But we can imagine. . .

I mean ... just statistically ...
There have to be planets which sustain life
So there has to be other intelligent life

What if one evolved
To where the government leaders are not obstinate
But are open and solve disagreements by compromise?

What if another evolved
To where the law makers are not arbitrary
But decide for the benefit of the whole?

What if another one evolved
To where the bureaucrats are not selfish
But are productive and efficient?

NEGOTIATION

Prioritize your wants and demands
As compromise is a certainty
But you want to give as little as possible

Listen to learn your opponent's goals and desires
Understand your opponent's strengths and weaknesses
Be able to argue his point of view as preparation

Let your opponent have his say
Without interrupting or arguing
Acknowledge his point of view

Explain the areas where your opponent is weak
Point out your own strengths
But emphasize your willingness to negotiate

Find the points of agreement to build on
Concentrate on objectivity
By taking personalities and emotions out of the discussion

You can show anger but not be angry
Or make an unreasonable demand
To throw off your opponent

Also if he wants to control, act submissive
If he thinks he is intelligent, act stupid
If he talks reason, act unreasonable

Keep time on your side
Initially spend more time arguing over minor points
So major concessions will be towards the end

If the process stalls
Be prepared to be creative with options

Give on a less important item but get a priority

THE TEN FUNDAMENTAL RIGHTS OF THE HUMAN CONDITION

TO LIVE IN YOUR OWN SAFE HOME

TO PROTECT YOURSELF AND YOUR FAMILY

TO BE RESPECTED BY EVERYONE

TO BE JUDGED EQUALLY BY JUST LAWS

TO HAVE AN OPPORTUNITY TO BE PRODUCTIVE

TO BE COMPENSATED FOR YOUR PRODUCTIVITY

TO HAVE THE OPPORTUNITY FOR LEARNING

TO TRAVEL SAFELY WITHIN YOUR COUNTRY

TO PARTICIPATE IN YOUR OWN GOVERNANCE

TO BELIEVE IN AND WORSHIP YOUR OWN GOD

WEST AND EAST

You are standing west
   I am standing east

You see the situation
   From your perspective
     And say you are right

I see the situation
   From my perspective
     And say I am right

You get angry
   Because I say I am right

I decide NOT to get angry
   But to walk west
     To get a better perspective

Will you walk east?

THE PEOPLE

The People live in villages of several hundred inhabitants
In a single lodge live the immediate family of parents,
　children, and grandparents
In other lodges live the extended families of aunts and
　uncles and cousins

There is a division of duties and responsibilities
The women take care of the lodge, household chores,
　and gardening
The men do the hunting, fighting, governing, and
　trading

The adults all take part in the raising and education of
　the children
The mothers with the girls and the fathers with the boys
As they grow the children learn to give gifts to their
　mentors in gratitude

Gratitude, generosity, and respect are the key elements
　of everyday life
The old, the poor, the disadvantaged are all supported by
　the people
Hospitality to strangers is also important

The People are grateful to the Creator ... or *Great Spirit*
For infusing Mother Earth with the necessities for the
　People to survive
Namely, food, shelter, good weather, security, health,
　wisdom, etc.

The hunters coming back first give meat to those in need
Each leader must have proven his generosity before
　being elected

Before being a shaman, he must first have given away all
   his possessions

Respect is shown to each individual and his or her
   differences
Respect is given to those who work hard and are
   productive
Respect is given to the elderly because of their wisdom
   and sacrifices

Leaders are elected based on their wisdom and skills
Decisions are made by consensus
And delegation is important in carrying out
   responsibilities

The People believe in suffering as an opportunity to open
   their minds
Thus fasting and meditation are encouraged in order to
   be an adult
Individuals generally identify with one of nature's
   animals or elements

Every living thing has a spirit and individuals have a life
   after death
But life is sacred to the point that wars are not waged
If the cost of human life is going to be too great

The Christian invaders called them ... savages

ALL MEN ARE CREATED EQUAL

Thomas Jefferson in his Declaration of Independence
Left out one small word ... *white*
"All *white* men are created equal"

He did not believe non-land owners were equal
He did not believe women were equal
He did not believe black slaves were equal

In the 1700s when a new nation was being conceived
The poor, the disadvantaged, the minorities, women,
Anyone who did not own land, could not vote

Thus women were not supposed to be educated
Because they could not own property nor vote
They had only one main purpose ... sex

Jefferson slept with his black slave girl, Sally,
For many nights, for many years
She had only one main purpose ... sex

Sally did not have a choice.
What is it called when an owner
Has sex with his slave? Rape?

Their children were his property.
What is it called when an owner
Has sex with a slave to produce more slaves? Breeding?

But Jefferson never emancipated Sally
Not even in his last will and testament.
He would have, if he had loved her

So as we begin the 21st century
When you recite the Declaration of Independence
Do you believe that ALL MEN are created equal?

TOP SECRET REPORT

A top government agency reports
That the space agency has found and is spying on
A planet that has intelligent life

The planet has one advanced civilization
Which manufactures all kinds of vehicles
Including those that enter space

This is important because this society is losing
    productivity
Through a lack of new births
And a desire of foreigners to immigrate

Without the ability to continue to develop
The research and the manufacturing
Of high quality goods and services

This society will decline
And eventually decay from within
Leaving it a target for a take-over by its enemies

The planet's strategy being developed
Is to kidnap foreigners without notice
And bring them back to work as "slaves'"

In monitoring this newly discovered planet
The space agency has determined
The beings call their planet. . .Earth

IN THE FUTURE

The Chinese have propelled their economy
And their military and space programs
To be the biggest and best in the world

In fact, they are the greatest superpower
Mainly because they have a terrible new weapon
A satellite with a powerful laser guided by video

This weapon can destroy a 1000-sq. ft. area anywhere
In a split second, a single blast can bring down a building
And all living creatures in a wide area would be dust

Now the Chinese have their own definitions
Of who is a patriot and who is a terrorist
But the innocents are just casualties of war

A Chinese dissident has set off a bomb
Killing hundreds in a government building
And escapes to the United States of America

The Americans welcome the dissident as a hero
And agree to protect him from the Chinese
The furious Chinese decide to use their weapon

Hundreds of Americans are killed, but there is no capitulation
The Chinese army invades several west coast ports
But still the Americans do not surrender

After thousands are killed on both sides
Neither the Chinese nor the Americans have an advantage
Both sides are forced to negotiate

If YOU were the arbitrator, how would you solve this?
You write up this scenario, but switch the words ...
So *American*s become *Chinese* and *Chinese* become *Americans*

I HEARD ABOUT THIS MAN

A while back I heard about this man
Who was sort of rebellious and different
Oh, what was his name?

He gave to the poor his goods and wealth
And encouraged others to do the same
Oh, what was his name?

He made fun of the wealthy
Because they would not be, when they died
Oh, what was his name?

He did not object to paying taxes
But probably was against wasteful spending
Oh, I don't remember, what was his name?

He did not like arrogant intellectuals
Because they were out of touch with reality
Oh, what was his name?

He thought most religious leaders
Were just plain hypocritical
I am trying to remember, what was his name?

Oh, now I remember
Most people now call him *Liberal*
To a few he is just *Jesus*

MY UNCLE BILL

My Uncle Bill is the successful one in the family
He is very wealthy and powerful
And has lots of friends

He is very generous
He says his accountant has to tell him
How much he can donate to charity

He is very well educated
He says, even though he partied a lot in college
That going to the right college was very important

He likes minorities
He says he would only use Mexican gardeners
And the black athletes are the best in the world

He is not a racist
He says he has forgiven the Jews for killing Jesus
Plus they keep the Arabs in line

He is very friendly
He has this loud booming voice
Which he says it's so people can hear him

He is very successful
He says that living in the right community
And going to the right church are keys

He is very patriotic
He says he votes all the time and it is easy
All you have to do is pull one lever that says: All Republicans

He is very intelligent
He says he knows what is wrong with the world
And if he were President he could solve all the problems

MY UNCLE TIM

My Uncle Tim is a great guy
We call him a *brainiac*
But he says he is just a critical thinker

He reads two newspapers a day
He says that they give him different perspectives
So that he can better understand all the issues

He likes politics especially voting
He says it is difficult when there are many choices
Because of the research and analysis

He is not prejudiced against anyone
He says prejudice is just ignorance
Because people fear what they don't know

He is very quiet
He says he only talks
When there is something important to say

He does not like to be constrained
He told me secretly that he likes to skinny dip
And does not wear any underwear

He likes to travel to foreign countries
He says it makes him more tolerant
And appreciative of what he has

He has lots of friends
He says he likes to listen to what they say
Because it helps him keep an open mind

A lot of people call him for advice
He says he does not give any advice
But instead asks a lot of questions

He likes Uncle Bill
He says he is funny and ...
Harmless, but I wonder sometimes ...

END OF A BUREAUCRACY

On a warm autumn early evening in 1244 A.D.
The great Mayan civilization began to crumble
As the last farmer, known as *Smart Fox*, left his dry fields
And walked slowly into the jungle,
A tired, angry, and frustrated man.

The tax collector had visited him in the morning
Demanding more food to support
The nobles, royal family, priests, and warriors
Even though he had no producing crops
As the dry season had been long.

The army hads recently returned from a battle with a neighboring tribe
With many casualties and his son was one of them
Yet the warriors had destroyed most of their enemy,
Killing the nobles, raping their women, and mutilating the children
But they did bring back gold jewelry for the royal treasury.

The priests' numbers had increased over the years
As the drought became more intense
Because they needed to have more ritual sacrifices of young virgins
To please the gods in order to bring rain for the crops
But this only decreased the population of farmers.

The nobles had grown richer and fatter
As the army's successes in growing the treasury
Because of increases in the taxes on the peasants
Forcing them to give up a greater share of their food storages

Leaving them destitute
One of the nobles saw *Smart Fox* walking into the jungle
Like so many of the other peasants in the months before
And he cried out to the others...the nobles, priests, and generals,
Who was going to feed them?
Who was going to provide the warriors, the virgin sacrifices?

ACKNOWLEDGMENTS

I would like to thank the following professionals for their help and advice in this project:

Danielle Lincoln Hanna with Sapphire Book Editing

Anne Morrissey, retired teacher of philosophy at Chico State University

Larry Jackson, publisher, with Heidelberg Graphics

Greg Johnson, web designer, in West Palm Beach, FL

Rafido, book designer, with francavillaraphael@gmail

OTHER WORKS by JEROME
ref: writingsofjerome.com

TAO TE CHING by Lao Tzu, a 21st Century English Interpretation

THE GOSPEL OF THOMAS, the original sayings of Jesus of Nazareth

THE WRITINGS OF JEROME, a legacy of personal reflections

www.ingramcontent.com/pod-product-compliance
Lightning Source LLC
Chambersburg PA
CBHW071725040426
42446CB00011B/2222